ydsole 509

W9-AAS-403

Start Mushrooming

The Easiest Way to Start Collecting 6 Edible Mushrooms

Stan Tekiela and Karen Shanberg

Start Mushrooming

The Easiest Way
to Start Collecting
6 Edible Mushrooms

Stan Tekiela and Karen Shanberg

Illustrations by Laverne Dunsmore
Cover Photograph by Tom Bernhardt

Adventure Publications
Cambridge, Minnesota
1993

© 1993 Adventure Publications
P.O. Box 269
Cambridge, MN 55008
All rights reserved

ISBN 0-934860-96-3
 Printed on Recycled Paper

Acknowledgments

The following people were indispensable in the writing of this book. In addition we'd like to thank our friends and co-workers who put up with our constant babbling and carrying on about this project.

And above all, our undying praise to the computer god.

Lee Muggli, for his *patience* from his hospital bed.
J.D. Jackson, Ph.D., for *Jacksonizing* our manuscript.
John Dunlop, for his *measured* help, thanks a billion centimeters.
Herb Harper, for *checking* our book.
Philip Mortinson, for your *life after death* contribution.
John Ratzloff, for *rooning* our manuscript.
Kathy Heidel, who got the *puffball!* rolling.
Kevin Doyle, of *Forest Mushroom, Inc.* for sharing his bounty.
Rob Youcha, *you* know why.
Andrea McGillan, thanks for the *use* of your son.
Bjorn McGillan, for your patient *hands.*
Elwin Stewart, for taking the time to *check our list.*
Irene (Joe) Meyer, for your *guiding hands.*
Neil Shanberg for your *support.*
Hazel Retzlaff, for *editing* our manuscript.

And to the following cooks for sharing their recipes:

Ralph and Diane Anderson
Krista and Joe Alper
Teresa Claps
Fireman Kooty
Adele Martin
Stan Tekiela, Sr.
Brad Ryti
Katherine Tekiela

Dedication

To my father who first inspired and to my mother who always supported me in all of my interests, this book is dedicated to you.

Stan

To my parents whose loving support of my choices and pursuits has been their greatest gift.

Karen

Think Metric

We invite our readers to begin to think metric with the metric
measurement references included throughout the text. Meters
and liters are used worldwide and by the scientific community
in the United States. Based on ten, you can go from one unit of
measurement to the next without converting, just move a
decimal point; no need to memorize. Don't convert. Just
measure with metric until you become comfortable with each
unit. Practice. It's amazing to discover that puffballs can be 30
centimeters wide.

Table of Contents

If you follow your bliss, you put yourself on a kind of track that has been there all the while, waiting for you, and the life that you ought to be living is the one you are living. Wherever you are - if you are following your bliss, you are enjoying that refreshment, that life within you, all the time.

Joseph Campbell

Foreword

Did you ever want to go out and pick mushrooms for a meal but you didn't for fear of not knowing which were poisonous? I've known the feeling. Have you looked at mushroom field guides and felt overwhelmed by the number of species? I've experienced that, too. So how do you get started? With *Start Mushrooming*.

Karen and Stan set out to make the world of mushrooms as easy and enjoyable as possible. Starting with only six of the most common and easily-recognized mushrooms, and a unique "check-off" guide, you can safely and confidently learn to identify these mushrooms. You don't need my background as a mycologist to safely collect edible mushrooms. Safe mushroom hunters learn to correctly identify a few edible species and stay within their knowledge. Leave the experimenting to the foolhardy.

Start by learning a few mushrooms well, and then add more each season. Soon you will know enough to take advantage of nature's bountiful fungal produce, most of which is never harvested, as the eminent mycologist C.D. Badham said at the beginning of the last century in *The Spurned Harvest*:

> *"Whole hundredweights of rich, wholesome diet rotting under the trees; woods teaming with food and not one hand to gather it; and this, perhaps, in the midst of poverty and all manner of privations and public prayers against imminent famine."*

Although this was written about two hundred years ago, attitudes towards mushrooms have changed very little.

Start Mushrooming will make you a safe mushroomer. It goes beyond merely matching a picture with a fresh specimen. The check-off guide for mushroom identification helps you start off on the right foot. The key features in the check-off guide are the same as those in more complicated field guides, but the check-off guide is much easier to use.

A little knowledge could be a dangerous thing, but not if one does not go beyond the limits of one's knowledge. *If you cannot positively identify a mushroom, don't take a chance by eating it.* By operating within your range of knowledge, you'll stay out of trouble.

It's difficult to find a hobby that doesn't require a large investment, but mushrooming requires few supplies. It's an interesting and enjoyable way to add to the pleasure of walking in the woods, increasing your larder at the same time.

The mushroom recipes in this book are delicious. There is not just one mushroom flavor; many have very distinct and unique flavors and aromas. These recipes enhance them all.

Stan and Karen provide a rich blend of enthusiasm and an environmentally-conscious approach to the art of mushrooming. They delight in sharing their experiences with those anxious to develop this new skill. Their easy approach will guide you safely and confidently into the world of mushrooms.

Happy Mushrooming!

Lee M. Muggli
Past-president of the Minnesota Mycological Society and
Vice-president of the North American Mycological Association

Introduction

Have you ever walked through the woods, seen mushrooms
growing and reminisced about grandparents who gathered
mushrooms for the table? Did you wonder how they gained that
knowledge and where that knowledge has gone? In just one or
two generations, we seem to have lost this information that
historically was passed from generation to generation. *Start
Mushrooming* hopes to reconnect you with the tradition of
mushroom hunting and at the same time, help you experience a
fascinating part of the natural world. Once you delight in discovering a patch of morels or prepare a dish of oyster mushrooms for the family, you'll never want to let go of the tradition
again.

Many mushroom books are available, but this one is unique
because it focuses on helping the novice begin. Other guides
often list scores of mushrooms with just as many illustrations,
photos and descriptions. They assume you have found a mushroom and then hope you can identify it by comparing it to
hundreds of pages of information in the book. *Start Mushrooming,* however, wants you to start in your living room by first
reading about when, where, why and how to begin looking for a
select group of six edible, easy-to-identify mushrooms. These
mushrooms were selected because they have several distinct
characteristics and are unlikely to be confused with any others.
A pro-active approach such as this sends you out on a specific
search and therefore increases the likelihood of your success.
We have chosen six unmistakable edible mushrooms to keep

your hunt easy, focused and safe. We have kept the book simple and to the point. By using our easy "check-off" guide, photos and illustrations, we will guide you to the correct mushroom every time. Once you know what to look for, avoiding a poisonous mushroom will be as easy as differentiating between a swan and a robin. You'll discover how simple it is to *Start Mushrooming.*

Besides wanting to provide an easy mushroom-hunting resource that introduces novices to the pleasures of finding, collecting, preserving and eating wild mushrooms, we also want to help influence environmental awareness. The more we experience the outdoors and feel connected to the plant and animal worlds, the more we will realize we are all part of one earth, and we'll make better choices concerning it.

Welcome to the world of mushrooming.

Enjoy the wild,

Stan and Karen

Start
Mushrooming

Morel Quest

The madness overtakes you,
It creeps into your mind.

It's an all-consuming feeling,
A quest that happens all the time.

The quest begins in spring or summer,
Depending on where you live.

Search under last year's foliage,
Your fingers as the sieve.

Look beneath the passing elms
Right after the life–giving rains.

Search high in the apple orchards,
Search low on river banks

For the elusive morel,
And then give thanks –

Thanks to our loving earth.

Katherine A. Tekiela

Before You Begin

Two unique features of this book are: 1) we have focused on only six edible mushrooms that are easy for the novice to identify; and 2) we have developed a check-off guide for each of the six to ensure easy and positive identification. By answering six yes/no questions about the characteristics of each mushroom, you'll confirm its identity. The questions relate to:

Season • Habitat • Appearance
Cap • Gills • Stem

While it may be tempting to go right to the check-off guide and head for the woods, it's very important that you don't. Accurate background information is necessary and can be gained by using the book as it is laid out.

Learn what a mushroom is, how it develops and the terminology for its parts. You'll need this background to use the check-off guide.

Learn how, when and where to hunt.

Learn the basics of collecting.

Before you leave the house, learn about poisonous mushrooms. The best defense is a good offense.

Become familiar with the check-off guide and how it works.

Chapter 1 Before You Begin

Read about each of the selected six edible mushrooms. Study the text, check-off guide, photo and illustration. In subsequent seasons, after some experience in using all the information provided, you may only need to refer to the quick seasonal review that follows the text.

Do all the reading first. Then focus your hunt and take this book along. Once you've found your treasure, compare your specimen to the text, photos and illustrations. Then, for positive identification, go through the check-off guide. If you can assuredly answer "yes" to each of the six characteristics, you have the right mushroom. After completing the check-off, take one final look at the illustrations and color photograph to confirm the identification.

Harvest according to the rules suggested. Bring home the bounty and use the delicious recipes to enhance and embellish the experience. We'll guarantee you've discovered a new passion!

General Cautions

There are many edible wild mushrooms other than the six we have selected for this book. Until you take a course or you are gathering with a mushroom expert, don't collect any mushrooms for eating other than the six that have been outlined here.

To add to your knowledge about mushrooms, you may want to take an identification class, join your local mycological society or attend mushroom hikes sponsored by your local nature center.

When collecting mushrooms in the fall, be familiar with local deer and small game hunting seasons and avoid hunting zones or wear bright orange clothing. When collecting on private property always obtain the owner's permission. It may help to offer some of the bounty for their kindness. State and national parks don't allow the collection of plants, but many will allow mushroom collection. Check with the park rangers or manager to get permission. Remember, you represent mushroom hunters across the country, so use good judgement when on public and private lands. You'll be surprised just how many people are interested in wild mushrooms; be ready to answer questions.

If you go mushroom hunting alone, tell someone where you will be and when you may be expected to return. Learn to recognize and treat poison ivy if you are unfortunate enough to encounter it. Wear long pants and a hat to protect against insects and the sun. A walking stick is helpful in many situations and can be fashioned from nearly any stick. Now you're ready to learn how to *Start Mushrooming!*

Dunsmore '92

My father
placed his hand on
my shoulder to suggest we
should slow down. In a soft
voice I could hear him say, "This
is the place. Keep a sharp eye." Our
dog ran ahead wildly. She had no interest in
wild mushrooms; it was the scent of the woods that guided her.

Even though many years have passed, I can still hear my
father's voice echo in the forest breeze, always present and
guiding as if he were still by my side. And as long as I forage
these woods, I know he always will be.

Chapter 2

Mushroom Lingo
What is a Mushroom?

So what is a mushroom? This question is easy to answer in technical terms, but the trick is to translate the scientific terms into commonly accepted words. First, mushrooms are not members of the plant kingdom because they don't function like plants or have similar structures. Referring to mushrooms as plants is technically wrong. Don't fall into this trap. Secondly, we use the word "mushroom" throughout this book when technically we are talking about "fungus." "Mushroom" is the most common and widely-accepted term used to refer to the fruiting body of a fungus. It may help to think of picking a mushroom as you would pick an apple from a tree; both are a reproductive structure. Unlike the tree, the vegetative part of the fungus that produces the mushroom is generally not visible because it grows as tiny threads within the soil or wood. That's why mushrooms have had such a mysterious past. People thought they just popped up overnight and didn't understand that the vegetative part of the mushroom had been growing there all along.

The cap is generally the top of the mushroom and

comes in many sizes, shapes and colors, as you can see by the two illustrations on the preceding page. The technical word for the cap is "pileus" and refers to a hat or cap worn by ancient Romans. You may immediately think of the dome-shaped cap you've seen on a typical store-bought mushroom, but several of the safe six mushrooms don't have a clearly defined cap. The cap can be flat and semicircular as in the oyster mushroom, or cone-shaped with many pits and ridges as in the morel. In any case, the cap is the uppermost portion of the mushroom and is immediately above the gills or pores.

Although not all mushrooms have gills, in gilled species the gills are found under the cap. They are thin, blade-like, radiating structures, much like pages in a book. On the surface of the gills the microscopic spores are produced and released for reproduction. Spores are the mushroom's version of seeds. By a variety of methods, the gills release millions of microscopic spores into the air. Some mushrooms have pores (tiny holes) in place of gills that serve the same purpose. Some mushrooms don't have obvious gills or pores but produce their spores within the mushroom, as the puffball does. Distinguishing between these types is easy because the check-off guide asks, "Gills: present or absent?" and the choice will be obvious.

The stem or stalk is technically called a stipe. Although it doesn't carry nutrients like the stem of a green plant, it shares the same common name. Stems can be thick or thin, brittle or fibrous and attach to the cap in a variety of ways. A common attachment point is at the center of the cap, but stems can also attach at the side or edge. Many mushrooms don't have a stem because the caps are attached directly to the growing surface.

Regardless of the attachment, stems have one function: to get the cap up into the air to release the spores.

As the mushroom matures, it casts off millions of spores to be carried away on the wind. If a spore lands in a suitable place, it will produce a small thread-like structure called a hyphae, which will grow into a thread-like network called mycelium, the vegetative portion of the fungus where the mushroom will be produced. Then the cycle starts over, assuring that there will be more for the next generation of mushroom hunters to *Start Mushrooming.*

The small group of mush-
room hunters had been searching Mystic Valley for three
days without success. The
spirits of the hunters had
plummeted. If only they could
locate their mushroom treasure. Two days passed before
they discovered any trace. A faint pleasant aroma radiated
from all around. Knowing that air currents travel from low to
high elevations the group began their descent with a renewed
enthusiasm. "This must be the spot, the smell is so strong,"
someone said. As the group spread out some fell to their knees
for a better vantage point. A cry rang out, "I've found them!"

Chapter 3

Mushroom Hunting Strategies
How to Focus Your Search

Most guides concentrate only on identification and assume that the reader knows how, when and what to look for when mushroom hunting.

The most successful mushroom hunters are those who understand what a mushroom is and how it grows. You wouldn't search for morel mushrooms on the stumps of dead trees in autumn if you have knowledge of morels. Knowing the characteristics of each mushroom, such as in which season it occurs and in which habitat it grows, is critical to finding them. These characteristics are incorporated into the text and the check-off guide about each mushroom.

Let's start with the season. Mushrooms are seasonal so you need to know when they occur. If the mushroom you wish to gather appears in the fall, then it makes no sense to look for it on a spring walk. (However, if you happen across a good habitat for spring mushrooms, make a mental note to return in the spring.) Some mushrooms can occur in more than one season, and these are indicated in the check-off guide. While

Dunsmore '92

the season for any particular mushroom is consistent, the timing for the exact appearance varies from year to year, just as weather varies within a season. You might happen upon a mushroom while on a bike ride or a walk. This is a sure sign that the conditions are right and it's time to get serious about the hunt.

Mushrooms are 90% water, so moisture is very important to their existence. This is why most mushrooms occur in the spring and fall when most of the rain falls. The amount of moisture available prior to the season directly affects the exact timing of the mushrooms' appearance. You'll begin to notice that some years are better than others, depending on the rainfall and temperature. You'll want to hit the woods during a wet summer. Searching during or after an extended warm and rainy period is usually productive. Not only should you come up with more mushrooms, but you'll enjoy the deep, rich appearance of the woods at these times. Since most people stay indoors when it's wet, you'll have little competition and will enjoy the solitude.

If you haven't hunted a particular mushroom before, it will be helpful to spend some time studying the pictures in this book to develop a mental image of the mushroom, especially when hunting for morels, which are masters at hiding. Fix the size, shape, color and texture into a mental image so that your mind is more open to seeing the mushrooms you are collecting. Bring this book and refer to the pictures and the checklist frequently.

When hunting for mushrooms that grow on the ground, it is important to get down close to them. This reduces the angle of sight and will allow the mushroom to be seen. On family hikes, children can help search for mushrooms. They are closer to the ground and have an advantage over adults when it comes to spotting these elusive treasures. Find a likely habitat, then have them crouch down and scan the ground ahead of them.

Some mushrooms are well-camouflaged and can be easily missed by untrained eyes. A walking stick can gently move the vegetation in order to find those mushrooms that are hiding. This technique is essential in finding morel mushrooms. Most mushrooms in this book tend to be large and obvious and require only a slow walk in the woods to be discovered.

When looking for larger mushrooms that grow on trees or the ground, we find that using something called "scanning vision" works best. Scanning vision is looking at the woods in a sweeping motion from side to side without fixing your sight on any specific object. Look for shapes and colors that are not consistent with the rest of the woods. Scanning vision works well for bird and other wildlife watching, too. A good pair of binoculars will help to determine if something in the distance is a mushroom or just part of an irregular tree branch.

It is not important to have a large wooded area in which to hunt because mushrooms know no boundaries and will grow in urban and suburban settings. As long as there is a source of nutrients and moisture, the mushrooms will grow. Avoid lawns, roadsides, golf courses and areas that have been treated with herbicides and pesticides. Mushrooms absorb these chemicals and you would be ingesting them directly. As hunters of wild mushrooms we are again personally confronted with the way we are contaminating our environment. We can all become a stronger voice for a healthier planet.

An important factor in the success of the mushroom hunter is luck. Knowing how and when to look for mushrooms is essential, but a certain degree of luck helps.

Over time, you'll discover places that will become your favorite hunting grounds. Even though mushrooms seem to pop up overnight, the unseen portion of the fungus has been growing for many years and will continue to grow there year after year until the nutrients have been exhausted. Return each new season to harvest these delightful treats. We have many secret hunting spots that we return to every year. Like old friends, the mushrooms are patiently waiting for us to harvest them. In many areas of the country, the location of favorite hunting grounds is a well-guarded secret that hunters would rather take to the grave than tell. If a mushroom hunter does tell you where to look for mushrooms, it might be to keep you away from the mother lode or to send you on a wild-goose chase to keep you busy while they collect at the real location. In either case, the secret of the seasoned mushroom hunter is protected. Remember, when you *Start Mushrooming,* harvest selectively and with respect.

Their neighbor, basket in hand, was stooped over the soldier-like mushroom.
As they watched her fill the basket, concern
and apprehension grew on their faces.
With wrinkled brows they asked the inevitable,
"You're not going to eat those are you?"
"But of course I am," she grinned.
"Meet me back at the cabin in a half hour."
It wasn't long before they succumbed to the
aroma of Grandma's shaggy mane recipe and ate
their words for dessert.

Chapter 4

Plan Ahead for the Harvest

The tools for collecting mushrooms are not expensive nor difficult to obtain. Use a wicker basket with a handle or strap, or for large mushrooms, a wicker backpack. Plastic buckets are functional but wicker baskets protect the mushrooms while allowing good air circulation which keeps the specimens fresh. Don't use plastic bags for collecting; by the time you get the mushrooms home they will have started to decompose. A paper bag will serve well until you find an appropriate basket.

Use a knife to carefully cut the mushrooms at their bases so as not to disturb the mycelium. A medium-sized lock blade knife is the safest to use. Don't take all of the mushrooms from one area; leave some behind so that they may continue to cast off spores that will bring forth future mushrooms. It may be difficult to leave some behind, but it is an environmentally ethical thing to do.

Leaving some mushrooms behind is also beneficial for wild-life. Deer, squirrels and some insects, for example, depend on mushrooms as a food source. Look for branches in trees decorated with drying mushrooms left by squirrels preparing for winter. Squirrels often gnaw off the base of a mushroom and carry it up to the branches, wedging it between the twigs to dry.

Always cook all wild mushrooms before eating them! The cell walls of the sulfur shelf (and all mushrooms) contain chitin (pronounced "ky-ten.") Chitin can swell in the stomach and cause pain if it is not cooked first. It is important to understand that chitin is not a toxin, but rather a substance that is difficult to digest. To avoid excess chitin, collect only the fresh tender parts of any wild mushroom, and cook thoroughly. The same can be said for indulging in too many mushrooms at one time. As with any new food, eat wild mushrooms in moderation.

When you first *Start Mushrooming,* eat only one mushroom species at a time. Although these mushrooms are not poisonous, some people might have certain sensitivities to them. In the rare event you have a reaction to one species of mushroom but not another, you'll know which species to avoid in the future. Collect only fresh mushrooms, just as you would select only fresh produce in the store. Avoid any mushrooms that are swollen, bruised, wet, spongy, limp or obviously past their prime.

Do not collect unidentified mushrooms in the same basket as
edible ones. Small pieces of the unknown mushroom can get
mixed in with the edibles. Save the unknowns for another time
or a different basket. Before harvesting any mushroom, read
and review the chapter, "Confronting the Enemy: What About
Poisonous Mushrooms?"

When hunting and harvesting, take this book with you. You'll
want to compare the mushroom with the photo, illustration and
text provided. Go through the check-off list carefully to docu-
ment that each of the distinguishing characteristics is present.
You're soon to be a full-fledged mycophagist - someone who
eats mushrooms.

Upon finishing dinner the entire family sat down to let the fare settle-in, while the family cat helped herself to the leftover wild mushrooms.

"Shoo, down from there," came from the other room.

"She sure likes those wild mushrooms."

Forty-five minutes passed before the writhing and meowing began. They had never seen their beloved pet in such ill condition.

"If the cat is sick, then maybe it's only a matter of time for us!"

Within the hour the family found themselves explaining the story to the emergency room doctor. Stomach pumps were ordered, and at midnight the ill-fated family finally returned home.

"Someone should check on the cat."

Upon inspection, the group discovered six new additions to the family. Their cat had been in labor, not ill!

Chapter 5

Confronting the Enemy
What About Poisonous Mushrooms?

The best way to protect yourself from an enemy in any situation is to know all about that enemy - what it is and what it looks like. That's your best strategy as a mushroomer, too.

Begin learning the poisonous mushrooms a few at a time just like the edible mushrooms. Poisonous mushrooms come in many sizes, shapes and colors, but the most obvious group (genus) of poisonous mushrooms is the Amanita. The Amanita group contains some of the most deadly species. They are abundant and among the easiest mushrooms to identify as a group.

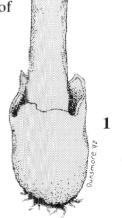

Learn to recognize the following four poisonous mushroom characteristics. A poisonous Amanita mushroom is indicated when all four of these features are present on one mushroom.

The four characteristics of the Amanita are:
1. **Volva** A cup-like structure at the base of the stem.
2. **Annulus** A skirt-like ring around the stem.
3. **White gills**
4. **White spores** A spore print indicates white spores (See illustration on page 39.)

37

The genus Amanita is responsible for most mushroom poisoning deaths. It is very important to learn how to identify this group of fungi and avoid collecting any mushrooms with these characteristics. Amanita are large, inviting mushrooms that grow in woodlands and are most abundant in the fall. How ironic that these deadly mushrooms are a favorite subject of outdoor photographers and are commonly used to illustrate children's books.

The common names for two species of Amanita are "the death cap" and "destroying angel." Consuming even a small amount of either of these Amanita could be fatal. *Avoid them at all costs!*

1 The **cup** of the Amanita is a structure that initially appears like a small Ping-Pong ball or golf ball and looks like a "cup" only when the mushroom matures. The cup, which in the early stages contained the entire immature Amanita mushroom, is called a universal veil. As the immature mushroom within the capsule starts to grow and expand, the cap pushes upwards through the capsule tearing off the top. What remains is the bottom of the capsule that forms the shape of the cup. Often the cup is covered by the soil and is overlooked by the beginning mushroom hunter. *It is very important to fully examine any mushroom to make a correct identification.*

2 The **ring**, or annulus, is a membrane that attaches the edge of the cap to the stem and protects the developing gills. When the cap matures, it opens like an umbrella, separating the bottom edge of the cap from the annulus, leaving it attached like a skirt to the stem.

3 **White gills,** as a single characteristic, are not a reliable indication of a poisonous mushroom, but when found in association with cups, rings and white spores, they spell trouble. Having white gills is not a indication of the spore color.

4 **White spores** are the rule for the Amanita mushrooms. Spore prints are easy to do on any mushroom. Simply place the cap of the mushroom, gill or pore side down, on a piece of white or black paper and cover the cap with a bowl or glass. Allow to stand for 30 minutes to three hours; then examine the paper. Under the bowl or cup, air currents are eliminated and the spores that are cast off are deposited directly down on the paper. When enough of these spores accumulate on the paper they become visible. Spore color remains constant and is unique to groups of mushrooms. They can be very helpful when identifying unknown mushrooms.

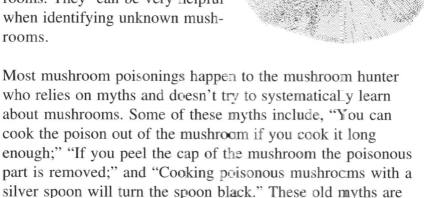

4

Most mushroom poisonings happen to the mushroom hunter who relies on myths and doesn't try to systematically learn about mushrooms. Some of these myths include, "You can cook the poison out of the mushroom if you cook it long enough;" "If you peel the cap of the mushroom the poisonous part is removed;" and "Cooking poisonous mushrooms with a silver spoon will turn the spoon black." These old myths are just that, and should never be taken seriously.

Chapter 5 Confronting the Enemy

If you suspect mushroom poisoning, call your local poison control center and seek medical attention at once! Some people can have allergic reactions to wild or domestic mushrooms. An allergic reaction is a reaction to an ordinarily harmless substance such as seafood or strawberries. About 15% of all Americans, and about 100 million people worldwide, are allergic to some substances. An allergic reaction to a mushroom is not a true mushroom poisoning, but it can still have serious side effects. Symptoms include runny nose, itchy eyes, rash and swelling of the tongue, or a full-blown systemic reaction that causes low blood pressure and unconsciousness. If you have food allergies, it is prudent to consult a doctor before eating wild mushrooms.

The best way to avoid poisonous mushrooms is to follow one simple rule:

If you can't positively identify it as an
edible mushroom, don't eat it!
When in doubt, throw it out!

At this point, if it's not one of the safe six mushrooms, don't try it. Save those mushrooms until you learn more.

Raindrops fall from his wide-brimmed hat, landing on a carpet of golden leaves. He has traveled this well-worn path for nearly a generation. Autumn has been the time to escape to the woods in search for edible mushrooms and this fall is no different. His only tools are a familiar walking stick and a tattered wicker basket. Heavy is his basket but light is his heart upon returning.

Chapter 6

How to Start Mushrooming
A Check-off Guide to the Safe Six

For each of the six *Start Mushrooming* mushrooms, you'll find text discussing each mushroom, photos, illustrations, a check-off guide and a quick seasonal review. The mushrooms are in order according to the season they appear, beginning with spring. The text for each mushroom contains natural history, lore and harvesting tips. This section is meant to inform and also inspire the reader to discover the real joy of mushrooming. Reading the text is essential to knowing the particulars of the mushroom.

Once you have sought out your mushroom by searching in the appropriate season and habitat, and you've matched a specimen with the photos and illustration, you are ready to use the check-off guide. The check-off guide is designed as a step-by-step process to confirm that the mushroom you have found is the correct species. Many mushroom guides ask for a spore print to make a correct identification. While spore prints can be very important, they are not necessary with these six mushrooms. The check-off guide points to the key identifying features of each mushroom and makes spore prints unnecessary.

The check-off guide is ordered from general to specific, so first note the season, where the mushroom is growing and its general shape; then look for the specific characteristics of the cap, gills and stem. For each listed feature, observe, compare and decide if the characteristic is present or absent. Just as a tree either has leaves that are needle-like or flat and broad, mushrooms either have gills or they don't. A certain combination of characteristics add up to a specific mushroom. Be sure that *all* of the characteristics are present before you gather. *If at any time you are not able to confidently check off all six characteristics, don't eat what you have found!* Sometimes mushrooms take on unusual shapes. To be on the safe side, don't harvest mushrooms that don't match all the characteristics, photos and illustrations in this book.

A Check-off Exercise

Here is a brief exercise using the check-off guide. You'll see how easy it is to tell the difference between mushrooms by observing their characteristics one at a time. For example, refer to the three drawings below and compare them to the abbreviated check-off guide on the next page. Examine the first mushroom and determine if the following features are present or absent. Do the same with the second and the third.

  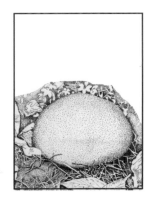

☑ Grows on the ground.

☑ Elongated, nearly cylindrical "oval" cap with many patchy scales.

☑ Single, straight stem

You'll see that only one mushroom, the middle one, has all three characteristics.

The actual check-off guide for each mushroom is more detailed and always examines six characteristics. Take the time to become familiar with the outline of the check-off guide on the following page. The more familiar you become with the features, the more focused you can be in your search Remember that only when you determine that all features are present can you confirm the mushroom's identity.

Quick Seasonal Review

For your first season or two as a beginning mushroomer, you'll want to comprehensively read all the information and study the photos and illustrations in this book more than once. In subsequent years and seasons, though, as you gain more experience, you may just want to review the information to refresh your memory, and then be on your way The quick seasonal review was meant for this purpose. It is not a substitute for reading, but it will highlight key information and when to find, where to find, how to find and how to collect each of the six featured mushrooms.

The Check-off Guide

☐ **SEASON**
Spring and/or summer and/or fall and/or winter.

☐ **HABITAT**
On the ground, or on wood.

☐ **OVERALL APPEARANCE**
Color, shape, size, presence or absence of cap/stem.

☐ **CAP**
Description of the shape and color.

☐ **GILLS**
Present or absent. Color of gills. Pores present or absent.

☐ **STEM**
Present or absent; how it attaches to the cap; hollow or solid; fragile or fibrous.

Quick Seasonal Review

WHEN TO FIND

WHERE TO FIND

HOW TO FIND

HOW TO COLLECT

Photographs

Morel

Morel - *Morchella sp.*; Morchellaceae family, page 56

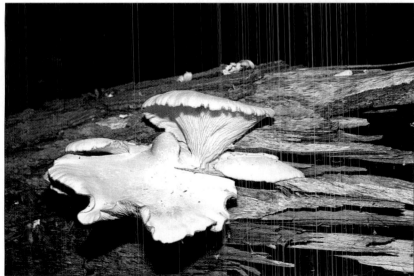

Oyster - *Pleurotus ostreatus;* Tricholomataceae family, page 62

49

Shaggy Mane

Shaggy Mane - *Coprinus comatus;* Coprinaceae family, p. 68

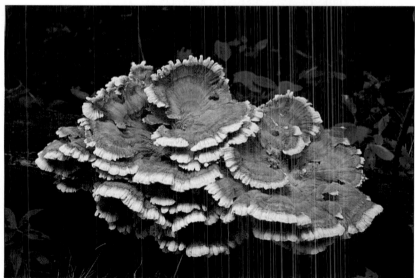

Sulfur Shelf - *Laetiporus sulphureus;* Polyporaceae family, p. 76

Giant Puffball - *Langermannia gigantea;* Lycoperdaceae family, p. 82

Hen-of-the-Woods - *Grifola frondose;* Polyporaceae family, p. 88

The Safe Six

Morel

The Jewel of the Mushroom World

Morchella sp.;
Morchellaceae family

Morel

Some people view the morel as the crown jewel of the mushroom world. It is certainly the most sought-after mushroom in North America. Springtime, and summer in higher elevations, is the season for a very contagious condition called "morel madness." It has been reported that ordinary people have turned into raving maniac morel hunters at the first sign of a new season. Depending on who you consult, there are as many as twenty species of morels in North America. Fortunately, all are excellent edible mushrooms. Yellow, Black, and White morels are a few names for the different species of morels. However, they all range from tan to black in color. They are sometimes called sponge mushrooms because of the honeycombed or spongy appearance of the cap. Morel connoisseurs will tell you that different species of morels not only look different but also taste different.

Morels depend on ample spring rains and warm temperatures. This is why south-facing slopes are the best hunting grounds; they warm up quickly in the spring. (A compass is a handy device for the morel hunter.) Inevitably, morels may be growing under the guard of prickly ash thorns. Going after these will be like giving blood at the blood bank, but without the cash payment. You may also find them in a patch of poison ivy. Morels do this on purpose! Be cautious!

Chapter 7 Morel

Once the morels have come up, individually they will last several days to a week depending on the temperature and humidity. The morel season itself lasts four to five weeks. If you are lucky enough to find a large patch of them it is a wise idea to collect only a portion of the available mushrooms. Leave the rest for others to harvest, and to allow the perpetuation of this coveted species.

Morel hunters use phenology to predict when the morels will appear (phenology is the study of the timing of natural occurrences throughout the year.) Depending upon which part of the country you are in, different signs indicate the beginning of the morel hunting season. One of the more widely-used signs in the east is when the oak leaves become the size of squirrels' ears. Some people use the blooming of lilacs, sprouting of the mayapple leaves or the flowering of trillium as their signal. Western morel hunters head for the hills the year after a forest fire. Getting in tune with your natural surroundings will help to be a more successful morel hunter.

Collect morels by cutting the stem with a knife or pinching it off at ground level. Always leave the underground portion undisturbed and healthy. Many times a new morel will sprout from the old site. Cut all morels in half vertically and inspect the hollow insides. Any mushroom with cottony material inside its stem and cap should be discarded. The morel's stem should be directly connected to the cap. All morels have a cap with pits and ridges and not folds and creases. If you are not able to check off the morel characteristics in the check-off system, chances are you have found a false morel. A false morel is a species of mushroom that looks superficially like a morel, but has a stem that is solid or filled with cottony material rather than hollow. The false morel should not be eaten.

Morels occur throughout North America. A good place to begin searching for morels is in forested areas and old apple orchards. Morels are likely to grow on and near flood plains of major rivers. Look for them just upland from low-lying areas. Another good morel-finding spot is around dead elm trees. This is often fertile ground for morels, but only for three to five years after the tree has died. The greatest crop will be produced the first year after the tree has died; it will slowly decline after that. It is unclear why morels favor dead elm trees, but it is a good place to start your search. Dead elms can be recognized by their v-shaped silhouette and bleached trunk. If you are having trouble identifying dead elms, check out all dead trees. Look around the circumference of the tree, out to 15-30 feet (5-10 meters.) Don't overlook small dead elm trees that have just started to shed their bark. To find them more easily, fix the image of a morel in your mind by staring at the photo provided. Crouch down close and scan the ground.

Huge flushes of morels occur after large forest fires. Search these burned areas the spring and summer following the fire. Note that the higher the elevation, the later the morel season occurs. Also in some western states, morels are known to occur under pine trees.

The time for collecting morels is only a few weeks each year. Don't let another season pass before you *Start Mushrooming*.

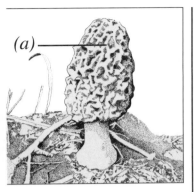

(a)

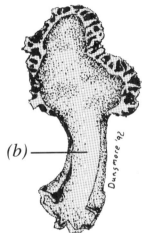

(b)

Dunsmore '92

Morel
Check-off Guide

☐ **SEASON**
Spring/summer.

☐ **HABITAT**
On the ground.

☐ **OVERALL APPEARANCE**
Sponge-like in appearance; tan to black in color; 2-6" (5-15 cm) tall.

☐ **CAP** *(a)*
Cone-shaped cap with pits and ridges; no folds or creases.

☐ **GILLS**
Absent.

☐ **STEM** *(b)*
Hollow like a straw; no cottony material inside; stem connects directly to the cap.

Quick
Seasonal Review

WHEN TO FIND
Morels may be found in the spring and summer.

WHERE TO FIND
Look for them around dead elm trees and old apple orchards, burned areas and river floodplains throughout North America.

HOW TO FIND
To find them more easily, fix the image of a morel in your mind, crouch down and look across the ground.

HOW TO COLLECT
Collect them by cutting or pinching off the stem without disturbing the underground portion. Slice in half to determine if the morel is hollow.

Oyster

The Seafood of the Forest

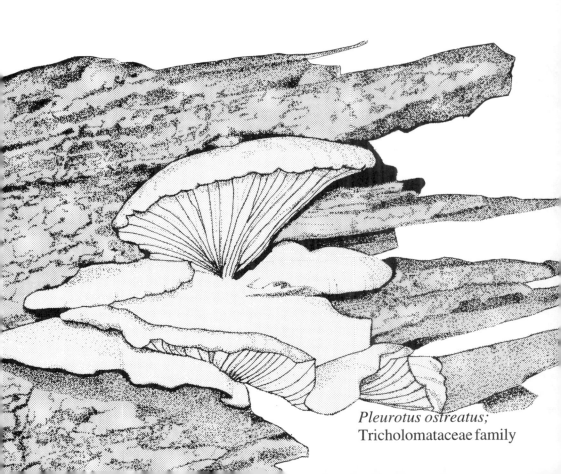

Pleurotus ostreatus;
Tricholomataceae family

Chapter 8

Oyster

The oyster mushroom takes its common name from the shape of its cap. The round clam or oyster-shaped cap has a rolled edge and can be pure white to buff-gray. When viewed from above, this mushroom is often described as "a clam attached to a log by its hinge." Its pliable cap is smooth to the touch.

Finding oyster mushrooms is not difficult because they grow in great quantities. It is not uncommon to spot a large cluster from your car while driving. However, the usual method to find oysters is to walk through the woods. A pair of binoculars is helpful to spot them in the distance. Rainfall is the most important component of the oyster's life cycle, so get out and search for them within one or two days after a soaking rain. In dry years, concentrate your search along creeks and rivers because of the available moisture.

Oyster mushrooms fruit in early spring and through summer, if the weather is favorable. However, they are more abundant in the fall. The oyster is so eager to fruit that sometimes a large cluster will emerge in the northern states on a warm winter day, only to be frozen that night. They may be harvested when frozen with a sturdy knife or small axe. In the warmer southern states the oyster fruits all winter with sufficient rainfall. Unless you plan to haul a ladder along with you on your hike, be prepared to tie a knife to the end of a long stick in order to get the ones that are higher than your reach.

Begin searching in a deciduous forest known to have a number of downed trees, the favored growing medium for this delicacy. Oyster mushrooms grow in large overlapping clusters or sometimes as a solitary mushroom on dead aspen, elms, oaks and maples and rarely on conifers. Oysters grow on the same log year after year, so when you locate a site, return during favorable weather conditions to check for fruiting. Take a large collection basket because a typical patch can yield several pounds. In warm weather the oyster decays quickly, so cook or dry your harvest as soon as possible. (See "Mushrooms All Year Long: Storing, Drying and Rehydrating Methods," page 117.)

The gills of the oyster mushroom are white and extend down to the attachment at the tree. An oyster's gills are so close together you can fan them like the pages of a book. Note that this mushroom has white gills like the deadly amanita, but not to worry - it lacks the other three characteristics. The oyster doesn't grow from a cup, have a ring around its stem or have white spores.

Harvest only soft and pliable oysters. As oysters age, they turn yellowish brown, droop and become inedible. Check for small insects that love the oyster as much as we do. Place your hand underneath an oyster cap and tap the top. A shiny black beetle may fall into your hand. This can mean you have found an oyster, but it also means that the beetles have arrived first. The beetles are easy to remove by hand or by submerging the caps in water. Some insects have evolved to live and feed on specific mushrooms. Be sure to gather only the mushrooms you can use and leave the rest for the insects and other organisms. Insects play a major role in natural food chains and need these places to complete their life cycles.

Despite its name, the oyster mushroom doesn't taste anything like seafood. In fact you'll find that they sometimes have a faint taste of anise, especially when collected from aspen trees. Generally this fleshy mushroom has a mild nutty flavor. You may find it on your grocer's shelves and prepared in restaurants since they are easy to grow commercially. Oysters can be grown at home from kits or in large-scale production using wheat straw, sawdust, coffee grounds or egg cartons as a growing medium. It's not as easy as throwing some mushroom spawn (mycelium) on a pile of tea bags, but many people have been very successful at culturing them. European cultivation of oyster mushrooms began in Germany after WWI and now they are produced in Asia, India, Taiwan, Australia and the United States.

Oyster mushrooms are one of our favorites. They are easy to recognize, great to cook with and very common throughout North America. They dry well for long-term storage and can be available all year long. They are a perfect choice for beginners. Purchase oyster mushrooms from a local super market, examine them for the characteristics discussed and then go out and *Start Mushrooming* for your own wild oyster mushrooms!

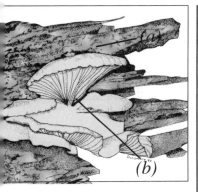

(a)

(b)

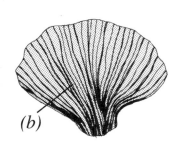

(b)

Oyster
Check-off Guide

☐ **SEASON**
Spring/summer/fall/winter.

☐ **HABITAT**
On wood.

☐ **OVERALL APPEARANCE**
Large clusters of cream-colored, oyster-shaped, overlapping caps attached to wood. Can have scent of anise.

☐ **CAP** *(a)*
White, semi-circular, fan or clam-shaped 2 to 6 inches (5-15 cm) across, can be depressed at the center with a thin, wavy edge.

☐ **GILLS** *(b)*
White, long, and thin extending down to wood.

☐ **STEM**
Absent; cap narrows to stem-like appearance.

Quick
Seasonal Review

WHEN TO FIND
Find oysters in the spring, summer, fall and winter.

WHERE TO FIND
Look for them on the trunks of deciduous trees or on logs.

HOW TO FIND
From a distance, use a pair of binoculars to scan for large clusters of white overlapping caps on trees while walking through the woods.

HOW TO COLLECT
Collect the oyster by cutting it from the tree without disturbing the mycelium underneath.

Shaggy Mane

The Edible Urban Mushroom

Coprinus comatus;
Coprinaceae family

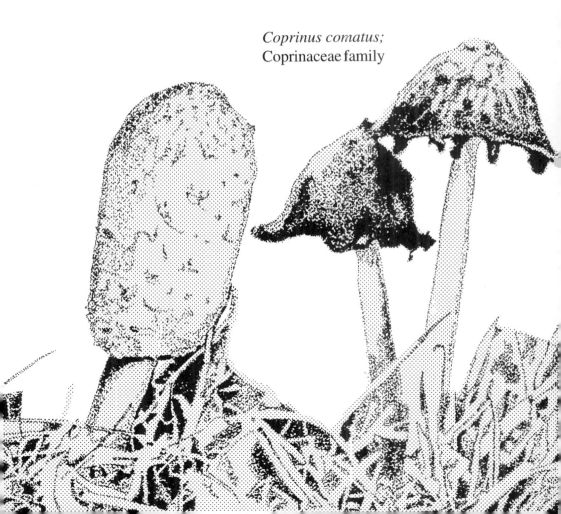

Shaggy Mane

The shaggy mane takes its common name from shaggy-looking patches on its cap. They are also called "lawyers' wigs" because they resemble the old fashion wigs worn by lawyers in colonial times. The cap and stem are white and the cap is covered with small brown and white scales. Scales toward the top of the cap are darker reddish brown and resemble a skull cap.

Fall is the best season for shaggy manes, but it is not uncommon to find them in spring and during a wet summer. Because they often grow in disturbed soils, they can usually be found along trails or playgrounds in your favorite park. They are also often found on newly-established lawns where black soil has been hauled in. Shags are famous for mysteriously popping up overnight in suburban lawns and, in fact, have been known to push their way through asphalt trails and tennis courts. This super mycological strength is caused by a natural hydraulic process in which the mushroom transfers water into its cells as it expands. It would seem that nothing can stop the shaggy mane from growing where it desires.

Shags like company; look for them in groups of up to 100. They are usually 2-6 inches (5-15 cm) high but can grow even taller. When young, the shaggy mane looks like a small white cylindrical mushroom cap growing

Chapter 9 Shaggy Mane

on the ground with the stem hiding within the cap. As the stem grows and expands, it becomes exposed and the elongated cap remains closed around the stem. The cap is filled with white gills and can grow up to 6 inches (15 cm) tall. (See illustration.) As the cap expands, the bottom edge tears away from the annulus, a "ring" that tends to be thin and flexible and slides freely up and down the stem like a washer on a bolt, unlike the ring of the Amanita which is directly attached to the stem. Because of the irregularity of the developing mushroom, a ring may not be found on every stem.

After the cap pulls away from the stem, the gills turn from white to a light shade of pink and then reddish brown as the cap begins the process of "auto-digestion." The shaggy mane belongs to a genus of over 200 species found throughout North America known as the "inky caps," and they all share one common characteristic: their caps liquefy in a process of auto-digestion called deliquescence, in order to release their spores. Shaggy manes also release air-borne spores before auto-digestion.

This decomposition process is fascinating. The gills possess an enzyme that initiates the process of transforming the edible tissue into an inky mess. The cap first becomes black around the bottom edge. As the mushroom ages over the next several days, the process of auto-digestion gradually moves up the cap until the entire cap is consumed. Only the cap is consumed; the stem remains intact. When mature, observe that the stem is attached to the cap only at the top of the stem and this allows the cap to easily separate from the stem when fresh. Often you will see only the stems of shaggy manes with rings of black ink outlining each stem. The inky mess is easily rubbed on the fur and feathers of animals or inadvertently eaten by animals as they graze on spore-laden grass. This transports the spores to new locations.

The base of the stem (at ground level) widens slightly but does not grow from a cup or volva like the Amanita's. To be on the safe side, examine the base for this feature the first few times you collect shaggy manes.

Shaggy manes will begin to turn to ink soon after collecting, so it is important to cook or dry them right away. One way to store shags is to sauté them in butter and seal them in a container before freezing. We have been successful in drying them, but only if they are gathered when they are fresh, before the auto-digestion process has begun. They must be dried in a food dehydrator with a heat source, so that they can be dried quickly and at a high temperature. Air-drying won't work; they'll get inky before they can dry out. Other methods of storing, such as submerging the fresh mushrooms in water or turning them upside down in an empty egg carton, do not increase the fresh life of shaggy manes. Fresh, frozen or dried, we find the taste of shags (caps and stems) to be outstanding!

During cooking, the cap will shrivel to a fraction of its former size, so adjust your recipes if you are substituting with shags. They also produce a great deal of liquid when cooking which makes them superb for use in soups and sauces. We like to simply saute them in butter with garlic.

A close relative of the shaggy mane is the "alcohol inky,"

Chapter 9 Shaggy Mane

Coprinus atramentarius. The alcohol inky differs from the shaggy mane in that it grows in tight clusters. Also, it is gray-brown, not white. The scales on the alcohol inky are transparent and are easily wiped off. Don't worry, both species are edible. The problem in confusing these two species of mushroom is that if you eat the alcohol inky and then drink even a small amount of alcohol, you may get an upset stomach with vomiting and heart palpitations. That is why it is called the alcohol inky. Depending on how much of the mushroom you eat, you'll need to avoid alcohol for one to three days. Avoid drinking wine with dinner or having an after-dinner cocktail if you are eating this mushroom. Without alcohol, the alcohol inky produces no adverse effects. With a little caution and common sense you can safely *Start Mushrooming* with shaggy manes.

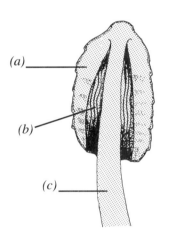

(a)

(c)

(a)

(b)

(c)

Shaggy Mane
Check-off Guide

☐ **SEASON**
Spring/summer/fall.

☐ **HABITAT**
On the ground.

☐ **OVERALL APPEARANCE**
Growing singularly or in clusters;
elogated "oval" shaggy white cap;
2-6 inches (5-15 cm) high.

☐ **CAP** *(a)*
White with shaggy brown patches,
cylindrical shape, rounded top; covers
most of stem. 3-6 inches (8-15 cm) tall.

☐ **GILLS** *(b)*
White gills tightly packed together. Turns
pink, then pinkish-red, then black with
age, bottom edge first.

☐ **STEM** *(c)*
Single, white, fibrous stem about 1/2 inch
(1 cm) thick, slightly enlarged at its base.
Stem attached to the cap only at the very
top.

74

Quick Seasonal Review

WHEN TO FIND

Find shaggy manes in the spring, summer and fall.

WHERE TO FIND

Look for them in open grassy areas, lawns, parks and along trails.

HOW TO FIND

The shag is an obvious white mushroom on a green lawn; look along trails and recently disturbed areas.

HOW TO COLLECT

It needs to be collected when fresh and prepared or dried right away before it starts to liquefy; dig up the base the first few times to be sure you don't see a cup (volva) under the soil surface. (See "Confronting the Enemy," page 37.)

Sulfur Shelf

The Chicken of the Woods

Laetiporus sulphureus; Polyporaceae family

Sulfur Shelf

If you have ever been out in the woods in the fall you have probably already seen this mushroom. We can't tell you how many times friends were able to describe this mushroom in near-perfect detail following a walk in the woods near a lake home or on vacation. This mushroom does not resemble any other mushroom and it grows in such abundance that it will become your favorite edible mushroom.

The sulfur shelf grows on wood and is never found on the ground. In rare cases when a section of wood is buried, a sulfur shelf can appear to be growing on the ground; in this case it looks like an orange rosette. It doesn't matter if the tree is alive or dead, standing or downed, log or stump - the sulfur will grow on it. The sulfur begins its growth as several small, bright yellow, finger-shaped growths that quickly expand to a large flat shelf or bracket. Each shelf or bracket is semi-circular and attaches directly to the wood without a stem.

The sulfur shelf takes its common name from its color and growth habit. The top side of the flattened bracket is strikingly bright orange. The outermost edge, or margin, is rounded and sulfur yellow; this matches the color of the underside of the shelf. The sulfur shelf is similar to the hen-of-the-woods in that they both have small pores beneath instead of typical gills. However, the pores may be too small to be seen without magnification. As the mushroom ages, the color fades to a dull orange and yellow. Just before it dies, the entire mushroom appears completely white, as though the color was washed out.

Chapter 10 Sulfur Shelf

The sulfur can occur in one single shelf, but most likely it will occur in a large cluster of many overlapping shelves. This is a very impressive sight. A group of overlapping shelves can span 2 to 3 feet (60 cm - 1 meter) along a fallen log, and is a favorite subject for nature photographers. Each shelf varies in size from 2 to 3 inches (5-8 cm), up to 2 feet (60 cm) across. The entire young shelf can be harvested. The large shelves yield tougher flesh and are less desirable as edibles. The outer edges of large older shelves are the newest growth. Use a long sharp knife to trim away this edible portion. Leave the portion of the fungi under the bark or wood undisturbed so that it may continue to grow. Any forester or tree surgeon would probably cringe at these requests because the sulfur shelf causes a red-brown heart rot in its host tree. This heart-rot will hollow out the inside of a living tree and cause the tree to become weak and die.

Depending on the amount of rainfall, the sulfur fruits from spring to fall. The sulfur shelf occurs throughout North America but seems to prefer different tree species throughout its range. West of the Rockies, the sulfur grows on conifers and deciduous trees. Elsewhere, the sulfur occurs on live and dead deciduous trees and even wooden decks. A word of caution: sulfurs growing on eucalyptus have been known to cause illness. Be on the safe side and don't eat these mushrooms. Once you locate a sulfur shelf, you are guaranteed a supply every year, providing the weather cooperates. The sulfur will continue to grow in the same place until it has used all available nutrients in the tree or log. It can take many years to use all these nutrients in a large oak or maple tree or log.

Sulfur Shelf Chapter 10

The sulfur shelf is also called the "chicken of the woods," (not to be confused with the hen-of-the-woods,) because of how this mushroom supposedly tastes. We think this is a misleading analogy because although the texture of the sulfur may be similar to chicken, it tastes nothing like chicken. The sulfur is considered to be a choice edible, meaning that it has exceptional flavor. We couldn't agree more.

As with all wild mushrooms, you should not eat the sulfur shelf raw. Collect the fresh tender parts and cook them thoroughly. A hint to determine the age of the sulfur: your fingerprints from handling will show on the surface of a young sulfur and not on an old sulfur. The sulfur shelf is an unmistakable mushroom for the beginner to *Start Mushrooming*.

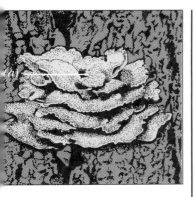

(a)

Sulfur Shelf
Check-off Guide

☐ **SEASON**
Spring/summer/fall.

☐ **HABITAT**
On wood.

☐ **OVERALL APPEARANCE**
Large cluster of bright orange
overlapping brackets or shelves. Sulfur
yellow beneath.

☐ **CAP** *(a)*
Fan-shaped or semicircular overlapping
shelves.

☐ **GILLS**
None; many pores (tiny holes) covering
the entire surface beneath; Pores are so
small that they cannot be seen without a
magnifying glass.

☐ **STEM**
None. Attaches directly to the trunk of
the tree.

Quick
Seasonal Review

WHEN TO FIND
Find the sulfur shelf in the spring, summer and fall.

WHERE TO FIND
It's commonly found on live or dead deciduous trees. In some areas may be found on coniferous trees.

HOW TO FIND
Easy to spot from a long distance due to its large size and bright orange and yellow color.

HOW TO COLLECT
To harvest young tender shelves, trim the soft outer edge of older shelves with a knife.

Giant Puffball

The Giant of the Woods

Langermannia gigantea;
Lycoperdaceae family

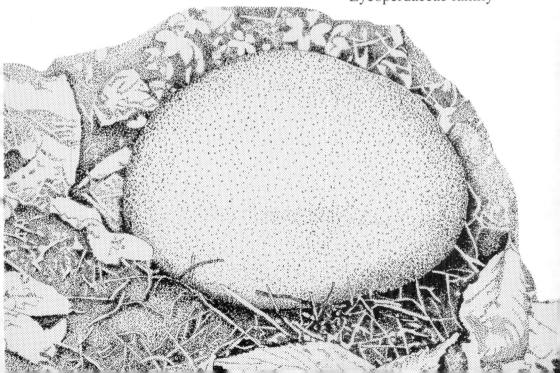

Chapter 11

Giant Puffball

The giant puffball is probably the best-known of all fungi and is the one most likely recognized by the beginner. Each time we speak with a "mushroom skeptic" we use the puffball as an example of a mushroom that nearly everyone knows. We get the same response every time: "I didn't know that puffballs are edible. I usually just kick them." We privately grimace from the thought of kicking this delicacy.

The giant puffball belongs to a large group of fungi that is referred to as "gasteromycetes" (meaning "stomach mushroom".) This reference comes from the spores of puffballs which are produced internally (like a stomach) rather than externally on gills. There are many fungi that are called "puffball" but we recommend learning only the giant puffball for now because it cannot be confused with any other mushroom. Giant puffballs have two acceptable Latin names, *Langermannia gigantea* and *Calvatia gigantea,* but *L. gigantea* is the preferred scientific name.

Giant puffballs are always found on the ground in clusters of two or three, or in scattered groupings. Look for them throughout North America in pastures, meadows, orchards, woodlands, golf courses and even on top of your compost pile. It is common for golfers to find what look like large swollen golfballs on the course throughout the season. Because all mushrooms readily absorb the chemicals commonly used to treat golf courses and lawns, avoid collecting in these areas.

When harvesting puffballs, be sure that they have the firmness, color and consistency of a marshmallow. Don't confuse golfball-sized puffballs with the young developing stage of the Amanita mushroom. (Review "Confronting the Enemy," page 37.) If you collect only puffballs that are baseball-sized and larger, there is no danger of confusing them with the Amanita.

The joy of hunting puffballs lies in the possibility of finding one that could easily feed your whole neighborhood. The giant puffball is one of the largest mushrooms, with record puffballs weighing in at 45 pounds (20 kg) with a diameter of two feet (1/2 meter.) Collect a puffball by cutting it at the base, or breaking it free by rocking it back and forth. Slice it through the middle. If it is snow white, firm and free from insect damage, it is suitable for immediate use in the kitchen. A small amount of insect damage can be trimmed away as you would do with garden vegetables.

All puffballs develop from a pinhead-sized body and may grow to the size of a basketball. As the puffball reaches maturity, the skin and internal flesh are transformed from the edible white consistency to an inedible pale yellow and then to olive green. Avoid puffballs that are becoming pale yellow because they may cause diarrhea. The green interior is actually the mature spores of the puffball. Spores are released through the skin as it cracks and peels during the aging process.

Few youngsters have passed up an opportunity to kick an aging puffball and marvel at the "smoke" that comes from it. Because the chance of one spore successfully landing on a suitable spot of soil is very low, this mushroom stacks the cards of reproduction success in its favor by producing copious amounts of spores. The puff of smoke is actually a reproductive insurance policy. We are not sure who took the time to count them, but the average puffball is said to hold seven trillion spores, with large puffballs reaching upwards of 20 trillion!

In early times, puffball spores and spider webs were mixed together and used as a coagulant to stop bleeding. Dried giant puffballs have been used as surgical sponges and as tinder for starting fires. Puffballs regularly grow to the size of a human head. Long ago in Europe they were said to be mistaken for skulls lying about in a field, hence their morbid French name, "Tete de Mort" (head of death.) Early European settlers in North America, familiar with European puffballs, used the same species of North American puffballs as a regular food source during colonization. Additionally, several Native American Indian tribes ate them as a substitute for meat, in soups and simmered over a campfire. A more modern way to prepare puffballs is to cut a slice up to an inch thick from the middle of the mushroom and fry it in butter like a large "mushroom steak," or cut into bite-sized cubes and fry. Try the recipe for Puffballs, Pasta and Peppers, found on page 101. If you love mushrooms, this is a must! The giant puffball is an easily-recognized mushroom and will make you happy that you decided to *Start Mushrooming.*

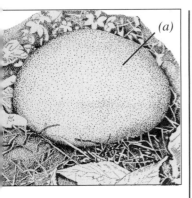
(a)

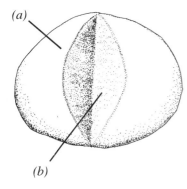
(a)

(b)

Giant Puffball
Check-off Guide

☐ **SEASON**
Summer/fall.

☐ **HABITAT**
On the ground.

☐ **OVERALL APPEARANCE**
In groups or singularly, 2-12 inches
(5-30 cm) in diameter, buff white, `
round or nearly so, as large as a basket
ball.

☐ **CAP** *(a)*
Large, round, irregularly smooth white
thin skin.

☐ **GILLS** *(b)*
None. Solid white interior, no structure
of any kind within.

☐ **STEM**
None; occurs directly on the ground,
might have a cord-like "root" underneath.

Quick
Seasonal Review

WHEN TO FIND
Find giant puffballs in the summer and fall.

WHERE TO FIND
Look for them on the ground in open fields and woodlands;
also along roads and railroad tracks.

HOW TO FIND
Look for large white "rocks" in open fields after heavy rains.

HOW TO COLLECT
Collect by cutting with a knife level to the ground, or rock the
whole mushroom gently from side to side to break it free from
the ground. Slice vertically to examine for: *a*) insects; *b*) solid
white flesh; *c*) no stem, cap or similar structure. (See "Confronting the Enemy," page 37.)

Hen-of-the-Woods

A Woodland's Wonder

Grifola frondosa; Polyporaceae family

Hen-of-the-Woods

The hen-of-the-woods is considered one of the choicest edible mushrooms in eastern United States, not only for its excellent taste but also for its large size. That is why each fall thousands of mushroom hunters take to the woods with a stout knife and a large basket. The hen-of-the-woods can become very large, about 12 to 36 inches (30-90 cm) in diameter, making it easy to spot from a distance. A typical hen tops out at about 10 pounds (5 kg.), but reports of up to 100 pounds (30 kg) are not uncommon. *100 pounds* is not a typo!

Typically a hen-of-the-woods occurs alone, but lucky mushroom hunters sometimes find several growing at the base of an old oak tree. Each mushroom is made up of a tight cluster of many spoon-shaped caps and stems. Upon close inspection, you will discover that the hen-of-the-woods grows from one central stalk and branches to many smaller stems. Each smaller stem attaches to the side (laterally) of each cap. The caps are light gray to brown, and without too much imagination can appear to look like the feathers of a hen, hence its common name. Each cap is from 3/4" to 2" (2-5 cm) wide. If you have ever seen a hen grouse and the varying sizes, shapes and colors of her feathers, you have a notion of how the hen-of-the-woods looks.

The underside of the caps and stems are buff white and turn yellow with age. Notice that there are no gills on the underside of the caps. The hen, like the sulphur shelf, is a member of the polypore family (has many pores) and lacks gills. Instead, the hen has many small pores that function like gills to release spores. These small pores resemble the surface of a sponge. They extend partway down the stem (decurrent). The flesh is firm and brittle, white throughout and easily broken. A fresh hen smells as tantalizing as it tastes and is something to behold. Try the recipe for Wilted Spinach Salad with Hen-of-the-Woods Mushrooms found on page 98 and we're sure you'll agree.

Hens grow as far west as the eastern slopes of the Rocky Mountains, but their usual range is the deciduous forest of the eastern United States and Canada. Depending on the region you live in, the hen-of-the-woods is sometimes called "sheep's head." Interchangeable common names can be confusing, so it makes sense to learn and use the scientific names for certain references. The old Latin name for hen-of-the-woods is *Polyporus frondosus;* in newer texts it will be referred to by its new name, *Grifola frondosa.*

Like an old reliable friend, the hen-of-the-woods can be counted on to fruit at the same location year after year. Most mushroom hunters have a favorite spot they return to each year when autumn leaves start to fall. In fact the specific scientific name "frondosa" means "covered with leaves" in Latin. The hen-of-the-woods grows on the roots of deciduous trees, especially oaks. The hyphae of the hen penetrate the roots of the host tree, causing what is known as "white rot," and eventually damage the tree. This is an example of a parasitic relationship between a tree and a fungus.

Hen of the Woods Chapter 14

In Japan, the hen-of-the-woods is known as "the dancing mushroom" and is called Maitake, (pronounced ma-i-tak-e.) The Japanese believe that the hen possess a strong anti-tumor substance. They grow it commercially on sawdust for food and medicine. The hen-of-the-woods can also be found in many Italian super markets sold as the "Italian cauliflower mush-room."

Cooking with the hen-of-the-woods is a genuine pleasure! It lends itself to pickling as well as baking, frying and freezing. We highly recommend that you try the recipe for Marinated Hen-of-the-Woods found on page 113. A fresh hen-of-the-woods will last several days in your refrigerator, and responds well to the traditional drying methods (see "Mushrooms All Year Long," page 117.) This mushroom that will give you the confidence to *Start Mushrooming* on your own.

(a)

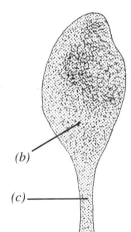

(b)

(c)

Hen-of-the-Woods
Check-off Guide

☐ **SEASON**
Fall.

☐ **HABITAT**
On the ground.

☐ **OVERALL APPEARANCE**
Large, round over-all cauliflower shape,
12-36 inches (30-90 cm) in diameter.
Multi–branched with many brown and
gray overlapping caps that look like
ruffled feathers of a hen crouched on the
ground, at the base of deciduous trees
(almost always on oak.)

☐ **CAP** *(a)*
Numerous overlapping and spoon-shaped
caps, 1-3 inches (3-7 cm) in diameter.

☐ **GILLS** *(b)*
None. Many pores (tiny holes) covering
the entire surface under the caps, large
enough to be seen without magnification,
and extending down the stems.

☐ **STEM** *(c)*
One central white stem that branches out
to many smaller stems. Small stems
attach to the side of the caps (lateral
attachment.)

Quick
Seasonal Review

WHEN TO FIND
Find the hen-of-the-woods in the fall.

WHERE TO FIND
Look for them on the ground at the base of living deciduous trees (mostly oaks) and stumps.

HOW TO FIND
Check around the base of living oak trees and stumps.

HOW TO COLLECT
Collect by sliding a large knife under it and cutting the central stem at ground level.

Recipes

Dunsmore '92

The butter twists and turns as it melts in the cast-iron pan. Strong earthy aromas rise from a basket of freshly-gathered morels. The marriage is only moments away. With a dash of garlic, the ceremony begins. Coated in butter and seasoned to perfection, the morels are the honored guests. Enjoy!

A Taste of the Wild
Recipes to Enhance Wild Mushroom Flavors

For your convenience, most recipes include amounts for both fresh and dried mushrooms. For directions on rehydrating mushrooms, see the chapter on "Mushrooms All Year Long," page 117.

The following recipes were selected to enhance the flavor and texture of each specific mushroom. Keep this in mind when substituting mushrooms within these recipes.

Wilted Spinach Salad with Hen-of-the-Woods Mushrooms

2 cups fresh Hen-of-the-Woods mushrooms
   ***or* 1 cup dried Hen-of-the-Woods**
5 oz. spinach leaves
2 Tbsp. vegetable oil
2 Tbsp. vinegar (flavored vinegar is preferred: Rosemary,
   marjoram, thyme)
4 Tbsp. honey
2 Tbsp. butter
Salt and pepper

If using dried mushrooms, rehydrate them in warm water for 30 minutes or until soft (see page 120); drain well. Wash spinach and arrange in salad bowls. Sauté the mushrooms in the butter. Combine the oil, vinegar and honey in a sauce pan; heat to a simmer and add the mushrooms and pan drippings . Pour the hot ingredients over the spinach and cover the bowl. Let stand for two minutes; serve warm. 2-4 servings.

Mom's Old-Fashioned Potatoes and Oyster Mushrooms

2 cups fresh oyster mushrooms
   ***or* 1 cup dried oyster mushrooms**
6 medium red potatoes, peeled and cubed
5 scallions or green onions, chopped fine
4 Tbsp. butter, divided

If using dried mushrooms, rehydrate them in warm water for 30 minutes or until soft (see page 120); drain well. Boil the prepared potatoes until soft. Sauté the onions and mushrooms in 2 Tbsp. of the butter. Drain the potatoes and pour them into the sauté pan with the onions and mushrooms. With a fork or potato masher, mash the potatoes until smooth. Add the remaining butter in small amounts. Extra butter may be added as needed. 2-4 servings.

Note: These potatoes will not be smooth in texture, but that is the point of this old-fashioned recipe.

Stuffed Morel Caps

12 *fresh* morel mushrooms
6 Tbsp. butter or margarine
2 Tbsp. Parmesan cheese
Garlic powder to taste

Use only fresh morels. Cut the stems off the morel caps and chop the stems fine. Melt the butter in a small sauce pan. Add the chopped stems, parmesan and garlic powder to the melted butter; bring to a boil. Spoon the mixture into the caps and arrange in a baking dish. Bake in a preheated oven at 375° for 10 minutes. Serve hot. 2-4 servings.

Puffballs, Pasta and Peppers

2 to 3 cups fresh puffballs, cubed
   or **1 whole fresh, medium-sized puffball**
   or **1 to 2 cups dried puffballs**
2 cloves garlic
1/2 cup peppers: green, red or semi-hot
1 Tbsp. olive oil
1/2 tsp. basil
Pinch tarragon
2 slices bacon with fat trimmed off, fried and crumbled
6 oz. evaporated skim milk
2 tsp. cornstarch
Dash Tabasco sauce, optional
6 oz. cooked pasta

If using dried mushrooms, rehydrate them in warm water for 30 minutes or until soft (see page 120); drain well. Sauté garlic and peppers in the olive oil for about 2 minutes. Add mushrooms and herbs; sauté until mushrooms are cooked, then add bacon bits. Add 4 ounces of the evaporated skim milk, cook and stir for about 2 minutes on medium heat. Mix the cornstarch with the remaining two ounces of evaporated milk; add this milk mixture to the pepper/mushroom mixture. Simmer and let thicken for about 2 minutes; add Tabasco sauce if desired. Serve over pasta. 2 servings.

Fire House Chow Mein

2 cups fresh hen-of-the-woods mushrooms, chopped
  or **1 cup dried hen-of-the-woods**
2 lbs. pork butt
1 bunch celery, chopped
3 medium onions, chopped
1/4 cup soy sauce
1/4 cup black strap molasses, dark variety
1/4 cup cornstarch
Water
1 16-oz. can bean sprouts

Cube the pork and brown in fry pan. Move pork to a big pot.
Add celery, onions, soy sauce and molasses. Add enough water
to cover. Boil for 5 minutes. Let sit for 3-4 hours to marinate.
Reheat and simmer for 30 minutes. At this point, if using dried
mushrooms, rehydrate them in warm water for 30 minutes or
until soft (see page 120); drain well. Add mushrooms to pot
and cook for 10 minutes. Mix cornstarch with enough water to
make a thick paste; stir into chow mein and cook until thickened. Stir in bean sprouts and heat until just warmed through.
Serve over chow mein noodles with long grain rice. 4 servings.

Mushroom-Nut Pilaf

2 cups fresh sulfur shelf mushrooms
   ***or* 1 cup dried sulfur shelf**
1 clove garlic, crushed and chopped
5 scallions, chopped
1/4 cup chopped walnuts
1/4 cup chopped or slivered almonds
2 Tbsp. olive oil
2 cups brown or wild rice
Black pepper to taste
Dash Tabasco sauce

If using dried mushrooms, rehydrate them in warm water for 30 minutes or until soft (see page 120); drain well. Sauté mushrooms, garlic, scallions and nuts in the olive oil. Prepare rice as directed on package. Toss the sauted mixture and rice together. Season with black pepper and Tabasco sauce. 2-4 servings.

Tasty Tomato and Sulfur Shelf with Macaroni

2 cups fresh sulfur shelf mushrooms
   or **1 cup dried sulfur shelf mushrooms**
2 Tbsp. butter
2 cups elbow macaroni
1-1/2 cups tomato juice, or soup
Dash onion powder
Dash garlic powder
Salt and pepper to taste

If using dried mushrooms, rehydrate them in warm water for 30 minutes or until soft (see page 120); drain well. Sauté mushrooms in butter. Parboil macaroni in water (boil for only a few minutes) and drain. Add the macaroni to the mushrooms in the sauté pan. Pour in the tomato juice, or soup; add the onion and garlic powder. Simmer until slightly reduced and macaroni is cooked. Season with salt and pepper. Serve hot. 2-4 servings.

Fresh Shaggy Mane
and Vegetables

2 cups fresh shaggy mane mushrooms
  ***or* 1 cup dried shags**
1/2 cup cauliflower, chopped
1/2 cup broccoli, chopped
1/2 cup cabbage, chopped
1/2 cup carrots, chopped
4 Tbsp. butter
1/2 cup water, if necessary
1 pkg. instant chicken cup-a-soup
Pepper to taste

If using dried mushrooms, rehydrate them in warm water for 30 minutes or until soft (see page 120); drain well. In a large fry pan sauté the mushrooms and vegetables in the butter. Add 1/2 cup water if necessary. Add cup-a-soup mix; stir well. Don't overcook; the vegetables should be crisp. Season with pepper. Serve hot. 2-4 servings.

Morel Cream Cheese Spread

2 cups dried morels, chopped
3 Tbsp. butter
1/4 tsp. garlic powder (must use powder)
1 tsp. parsley
3 8-oz. pkgs. cream cheese at room temperature

Rehydrate morels in warm water for 30 minutes or until soft (see page 120); drain well. When rehydrated, morels look like coarse hamburger. Sauté in butter; stir in garlic powder and parsley. Remove from heat and allow to cool. Then sauté until all water boils away, about 3 minutes. Beat the cream cheese until fluffy; fold in the morel mixture. Refrigerate overnight. You may whip in some milk to make a dip if you prefer.

Mushroom Veggi Soup

2 cups fresh shaggy mane mushrooms, sliced
   or **1 cup dried shags**
2 medium potatoes, cubed
2 Tbsp. butter
1 18-oz. can veggi soup broth
9 oz. stewed tomatoes (1/2 can)
2 cups fresh or frozen mixed vegetables
1/4 tsp. sweet basil
Dash celery salt
Pepper to taste
Parmesan cheese

If using dried mushrooms, rehydrate them in warm water for 30 minutes or until soft (see page 120); drain well. Boil the cubed potatoes until tender; drain and set aside. In a large sauce pan, sauté the mushrooms in the butter. Add veggi broth, stewed tomatoes, potatoes and vegetables. Bring to a boil and add the seasonings. Cover and simmer for 20 minutes. Top off with Parmesan cheese. Serve hot with bread and butter. 2-4 servings.

Shrimp and Mushroom Stir-Fry

2 cups fresh sulfur shelf mushrooms, chopped
   ***or* 1 cup dried sulfur shelf mushrooms**
2 tsp. cornstarch
2 tsp. cold water
2 tsp. soy sauce
Dash Tabasco sauce
2 cups white or brown rice
4 Tbsp. sesame oil
1/4 lb. medium shrimp, peeled and deveined
1 small onion, sliced
1 green pepper, chopped
1/2 cup pineapple chunks

If using dried mushrooms, rehydrate them in warm water for 30 minutes or until soft (see page 120); drain well. Mix the stir-fry sauce: In a small bowl, combine cornstarch, water, soy sauce and Tabasco; stir until cornstarch dissolves. Prepare rice as directed on package. Meanwhile, heat oil to medium high. Toss in shrimp and onions; stir-fry for 2-4 minutes. Add green pepper, pineapple and mushrooms; stir-fry for another 4 minutes. Add the stir-fry sauce and toss just to coat. Serve on a bed of rice. 2-4 servings.

Mushroom-Stuffed Tomatoes

1 cup fresh shaggy mane mushrooms
    or **1 cup dried shags (this *is* the correct amount)**
1 small onion, chopped fine
1/2 clove garlic
1 Tbsp. olive oil
1 tsp. curry powder
Dash salt and pepper
1/2 cup shredded mozzarella cheese
1/2 cup cottage cheese
4 large tomatoes, tops and centers removed
1/2 cup Parmesan cheese

If using dried mushrooms, rehydrate them in warm water for 30 minutes or until soft (see page 120); drain well. Sauté the onion and garlic in the olive oil. When the onion is soft, add the mushrooms, curry powder, salt and pepper. Cook over medium heat until the mushrooms soften; *cook no longer than 5 minutes*. Remove from heat. Mix together the mozzarella and cottage cheese; stir in the mushrooms. Fill the tomatoes with the mushroom-cheese mixture and sprinkle with Parmesan cheese. Cover and bake at 375° for 25 minutes. Uncover and broil until the top is browned. 4 servings.

Fresh Spinach and Mushroom Fettuccine

2 cups fresh shaggy mane mushrooms, sliced
   or **1 cup dried shags**
1/2 lb. fettuccine or linguini pasta noodles
1/2 stick butter (1/4 cup)
2 cups fresh spinach leaves, washed and chopped
1 shallot, minced (can use onion)
2 Tbsp. butter
2 Tbsp. white flour
1/4 tsp. salt
1 cup chicken broth or veggie broth
Black pepper

If using dried mushrooms, rehydrate them in warm water for 30 minutes or until soft (see page 120); drain well. Cook pasta as directed on the package. Blanch the spinach in boiling water; drain, rinse and set aside. Sauté the shallots or onions and mushrooms in 1/2 stick butter. Set aside and keep warm. For the sauce: melt the 2 Tbsp. butter in a sauce pan; stir in the flour and mix well. Add salt and chicken broth; simmer gently over medium heat until thickened; avoid boiling the mixture. To serve, top the pasta with the spinach and mushrooms; pour white sauce over entire dish. Dust with black pepper. 4 servings.

Onion-Garlic Mushroom Soup

2 cups fresh puffball mushrooms, cubed
_or_ 1 cup dried puffballs
1 large onion, chopped
3 large potatoes, chopped
1 clove garlic, chopped
2 Tbsp. olive oil
4 cups chicken stock
2 cups fresh spinach leaves, washed
Salt and pepper to taste

If using dried mushrooms, rehydrate them in warm water for 30 minutes or until soft (see page 120); drain well. In a large sauce pan, sauté the mushrooms, onion, potatoes and garlic in the olive oil. When the onion and potatoes are soft, add the chicken stock and the spinach. Cover and boil the mixture for 15 minutes until the potatoes are well-cooked. Allow to cool. Pour soup into a blender or food processor and puree. Return soup to pan; bring to a simmer and add salt and pepper to taste. 4 servings.

Mushroom Fish Sauce

1 cup fresh oyster mushrooms, chopped
**   *or* 1/2 cup dried oyster mushrooms**
2 Tbsp. butter
1/3 cup chicken broth (or 1/2 bouillon cube)
1/4 cup lemon juice
2 Tbsp. shallots or onion, chopped fine
1 small clove garlic
Black pepper
4 to 8 Tbsp. softened butter
2 hot cooked fish fillets - your favorite kind

If using dried mushrooms, rehydrate them in warm water for 30 minutes or until soft (see page 120); drain well. Sauté the mushrooms in 2 Tbsp. butter in a medium-sized sauce pan. When the mushrooms are tender, add the chicken broth, lemon juice, shallots, garlic and black pepper. Simmer until reduced down to 1/3 cup liquid. Remove from heat; drop the butter, one Tbsp. at a time, into the sauce and whisk or whip until smooth. Pour hot over steamed or broiled fish. 4 servings.

Marinated Hen-of-the-Woods

1 cup fresh hen-of-the-woods, chopped
1 medium red onion, sliced into rings
10 drops hot pepper sauce or Tabasco sauce
1/2 cup vegetable oil
1/2 cup white vinegar
1 Tbsp. sugar
1 Tbsp. pimento, finely chopped
1 Tbsp. parsley, finely chopped
4 cloves garlic, minced

Use only fresh hen-of-the-woods. Boil the mushrooms for five minutes or until just becoming soft; cool. Mix all the remaining ingredients with the cooled mushrooms in a large bowl. Pour into glass containers and allow to marinate in the refrigerator overnight. Serve cold as a salad ingredient. 2-4 servings.

Morel Honey-Mustard Chicken

2 cups fresh morel mushrooms
  ***or* 1 cup dried morels**
2 Tbsp. butter
2 chicken breasts, boneless and skinless
4 Tbsp. Dijon-style mustard
2 Tbsp. honey
Dash celery salt
Dash sweet basil
Black pepper

If using dried mushrooms, rehydrate them in warm water for 30 minutes or until soft (see page 120); drain well. Slice mushrooms into strips and sauté in the butter. Wash chicken. Whisk the mustard, honey and seasonings in a bowl. Coat both sides of the chicken with the honey-mustard sauce. Bake in a preheated oven at 375° for 20 minutes or until the chicken is thoroughly cooked. Smother in morel mushrooms. 2 servings.

Notes

Notes

Chapter 14

Mushrooms All Year Long
Drying, Storing and Rehydrating Methods

All mushrooms taste best when prepared soon after collection. But you may have collected more than you can eat at one meal. Nothing compares to a plate full of freshly-rehydrated hen-of-the woods or morel mushrooms prepared for a special dinner party with good friends in winter. Preparing mushrooms for long-term storage is not difficult and takes very little time. You will value your dried mushrooms like gold!

We recommend air-drying your extra bounty. It is the method that best maintains the flavor and integrity of the mushroom. There are several methods of air-drying mushrooms. Choose the method that is the most convenient for your needs. We find that when it comes to drying large amounts of mushrooms, the simpler the better. Drying time will vary with the amount of moisture in the mushroom, humidity in the air and the size of the mushroom pieces that are being dried. Air drying works for all but the shaggy mane mushrooms; see page 71 for instructions on how to dry shags.

Before drying, wipe off any debris and trim off any dirt or rotten parts. Very rarely will it be necessary to clean the mushrooms with running water. Washing will not injure the mushrooms but might extend your drying time or add water to a recipe that doesn't require it. As with garden vegetables, a blemish on a mushroom may be trimmed and the remainder eaten. Avoid old mushrooms or those covered with unusual growth or color. Next, cut the mushrooms into manageable sizes and examine for insect damage. For those times when you want to dry just a few select mushrooms, simply place them on a well-ventilated windowsill out of direct sun. Our favorite method is to string mushrooms with a stout needle and strong thread, and then hang them up in a well-ventilated room or in front of an open window. A pleasant aroma fills the room and lasts for days as the mushrooms slowly shrink to half their former size. Drying time is several days to one week. This simple method is very effective for all but very large mushrooms. You can cut such large mushrooms into smaller parts and dry them by the string method. These strings of dried mushrooms have been used in expensive floral arrangements and can be used to decorate a den or kitchen until needed for the table.

For large amounts of mushrooms, using window screens is the most practical way to dry mushrooms. Simply lay the screens flat with blocks underneath to keep them off the ground and

allow air to circulate around all sides. Spread out the mushrooms so they don't touch each other, and allow to dry. The
screens can be left outside in a shady area, and away from
squirrels and other animals who might think you have left them
a treat. Drying time is three days to a week.

Another way to dry mushrooms is with a commercial food
dehydrator. If the weather is too humid to air dry, or if space
is a problem, a commercial food dehydrator may be convenient. Two considerations are: 1) they will generate heat in
your home so they may not be a good choice for summer; and
2) they consume energy while other more natural ways do not.
If you do use an electric food dehydrator, set the temperature
on the lowest setting for six to twelve hours.

You may wonder just how dry you want your mushrooms to be
for long-term storage. If the moisture content is too high, mold
will grow on the mushrooms during storage. If the mushrooms
are too dry, they will be brittle and powdery. A happy medium is
desired. The mushrooms should still be slightly flexible but not
spongy when done. They should also retain a pleasant aroma.

Making mushroom powder is one of our favorite ways to store
and cook wild mushrooms. Start by cutting fresh mushrooms into
small 1/2-inch (1 cm) pieces. Dry the mushroom pieces to a
hard, brittle condition. Grind the dried mushroom pieces to a fine
powder using a mortar and pestle or food processor. Store the
powder in a pepper shaker and use in cooking to flavor just about
any dish such as soups, stews and meats. You're going to love
this variation on wild mushrooms. Think of the mushroom
powder as concentrated flavoring. Season foods to your taste.

Chapter 14 All Year Long

How to Store Dried Mushrooms

Storing dried mushrooms is as easy as screwing the top on a glass jar. Just about any jar will do. We find that an antique jar stuffed with dried mushrooms makes a special gift or decoration. Be sure to label the jars with the type of mushroom and the date they were dried. These dried mushrooms will last many years when stored properly.

Mushrooms that have been dried on a string may be stored by hanging them in the kitchen next to the stove. Just break off the amount desired and rehydrate.

Rehydrating Dried Mushrooms

All dried mushrooms are rehydrated in the same way. Place the mushrooms to be rehydrated in a medium-sized bowl. Add enough warm water to cover the mushrooms. Use warm, not hot water. Let stand for up to 30 minutes. Small pieces will rehydrate faster than larger ones, so keep an eye on the process. You can test for proper moisture by squeezing. Each piece should be soft and pliable. Squeeze out excess water before cooking. Try using chicken or vegetable broth instead of water for extra flavor when rehydrating. If you use water, save it and use as a substitute in any recipe that calls for chicken broth or vegetable broth.

Freezing
An Alternative to Drying

Freezing mushrooms is the next-best method to drying. but first they must be cooked. Freezing mushrooms without cooking results in soggy mushrooms upon thawing. When a raw mushroom is frozen, the water within the cells of the mushroom crystallizes and ruptures the cell walls. When the mushroom is thawed, the cell walls no longer can support or hold water. The consistency of the thawed mushrooms is soft and unpleasant. To precook mushrooms, sauté them in a large fry pan using 2-3 tablespoons (30-40 ml) of butter per 2 cups (500 ml) of mushrooms. Allow to cool, and pour into a reusable freezer-safe plastic container. Be sure to fill to the top, eliminating as much air space as possible. Label and date it properly. The contents will be good for up to a year.

Congratulations!

You have taken the time to discover that learning to positively identify the safe six mushrooms is not difficult. You are now officially a mycophagist (someone who eats wild mushrooms,) and you are ready to make each outdoor hike a new culinary adventure without the worry of making a deadly mistake.

We know you will enjoy discovering new places for hunting these mushrooms as well as sharing the tasty recipes with your friends. *Start Mushrooming* will open new doors to yet another natural wonder. We hope that your appreciation of wild edible mushrooms will contribute to an environmental ethic in our country that includes good conservation practices.

If this book encourages you to learn even more about the world of mushrooms, contact your local mycological society. Their members can provide a wealth of mushroom knowledge and you'll enjoy meeting people who share your passion for these edible delights.

Follow your bliss and enjoy the refreshment that is *Start Mushrooming*.

Bibliography

Arora, David, *Mushrooms Demystified,* Ten Speed Press, Berkeley, California, 1986.

Christensen, Clyde M., *Edible Mushrooms,* University of Minnesota Press, 1981.

Devignes, Antoine, *How to Recognize 30 Edible Mushrooms,* Barron's Woodbury, New York 1977.

Harper, H. Herbert, *Harper's Mushroom Reference Guide and Checklist,* Harper Publications, Forest Lake Minnesota, 1985.

Lincoff, Gary H., *The Audubon Society Field Guide to North American Mushrooms,* Alfred A. Knopf & Company, New York, 1981.

Major, Alan, *Collecting and Studying Mushrooms, Toadstools and Fungi,* Arco Publishing Company, Inc., New York, 1975.

Mushroom, the Journal of Wild Mushrooming, Editor Maggie Rogers, Moscow, Idaho.

Phillips, Roger, *Mushrooms of North America,* Little Brown and Co., Boston, Mass., 1991.

Ratzloff, J., Jerry Petermeier, *Roon: A Tribute to Morel Mushrooms,* Cabin Publishing, Long Lake, Minnesota, 1985.

Biography

Stan Tekiela is a naturalist and writer who lives in Victoria, Minnesota, with his wife Katherine. He has a Bachelor of Science degree in Natural History Interpretation. Stan is a member of the Minnesota Mycological Society, the Minnesota Naturalists' Association, the National Association of Interpretation and the North American Mycological Association.

Karen Shanberg is a naturalist and writer who lives in Minneapolis, Minnesota. She holds a teaching certificate and a master's degree in Outdoor Education from the University of Minnesota. Karen is active in many environmental organizations, including the Minnesota Earth Day Network, the Minnesota Naturalists' Association, the National Association of Interpretation, Kids for Saving Earth, the Madeline Island Wilderness Preserve and the Earth Day U.S.A.

Stan and Karen conduct environmental education workshops on this book as well as *Plantworks,* an award-winning book that introduces beginners to 15 edible plants. For more information on presentations, call 1-800-678-7006.

Index